Paisley Designs

44 Original Plates

by Gregory Mirow

DOVER PUBLICATIONS, INC.
New York

Published in Canada by General Publishing Company, Ltd., 30 Lesmill Road, Don Mills, Toronto, Ontario.
Published in the United Kingdom by Constable and Company, Ltd., 10 Orange Street, London WC2H 7EG.

Paisley Designs: 44 Original Plates is a new work, first published by Dover Publications, Inc., in 1989.

DOVER *Pictorial Archive* SERIES

This book belongs to the Dover Pictorial Archive Series. You may use the designs and illustrations for graphics and crafts applications, free and without special permission, provided that you include no more than four plates in the same publication or project. (For permission for additional use, please write to Dover Publications, Inc., 31 East 2nd Street, Mineola, N.Y. 11501.)

However, republication or reproduction of any illustration by any other graphic service whether it be in a book or in any other design resource is strictly prohibited.

Manufactured in the United States of America
Dover Publications, Inc., 31 East 2nd Street, Mineola, N.Y. 11501

Library of Congress Cataloging-in-Publication Data

Mirow, Gregory.
    Paisley designs : 44 original plates / by Gregory Mirow.
        p.   cm.—(Dover pictorial archive series) (Dover design library)
    ISBN 0-486-25987-0
    1. Paisley design—Themes, motives. 2. Arabesques—Themes, motives.
3. Textile design—Themes, motives. I. Title. II. Series. III. Series:
Dover design library.
NK1575.M57   1989
745.4—dc19   88-32714
                                                                      CIP

Publisher's Note

THE PAISLEY MOTIF derives its name from the town of Paisley in Scotland, where, in the nineteenth century, machine-woven woolen shawls were manufactured to imitate the luxurious, extremely expensive Indian shawls that were imported from Kashmir. The comma-shaped designs originated with the Moghuls; what they represent is not certain. Because the motif is capable of tremendous variety in form and in color (from subtle, muted tones to the most vibrant combinations), it has been favored by designers for use in textiles and graphics projects. Gregory Mirow has created an anthology of original designs that encompasses both the traditional forms of the paisley and modern interpretations that demonstrate its versatility.

1

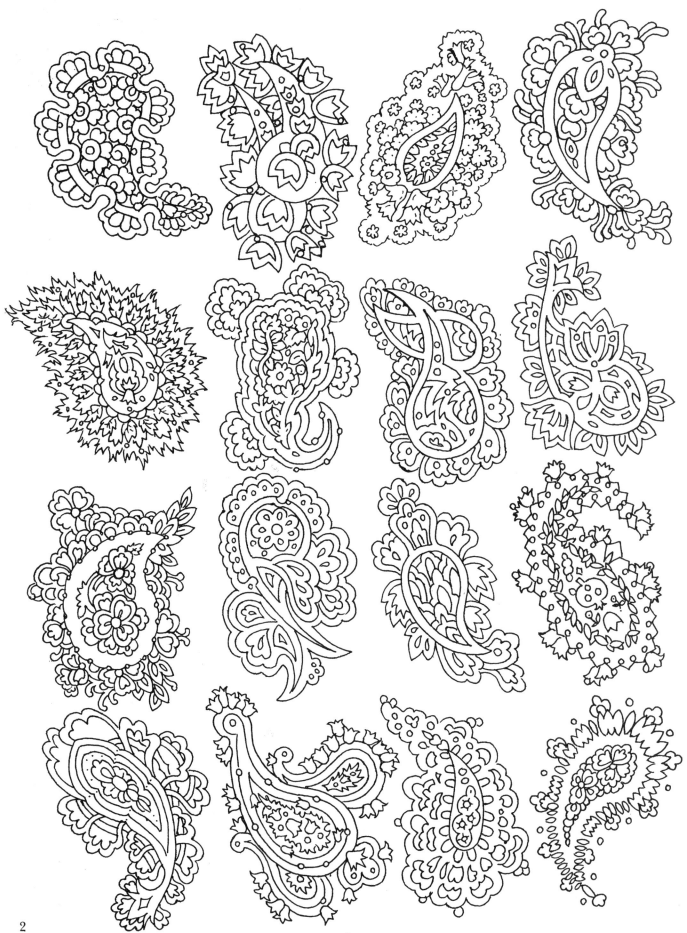

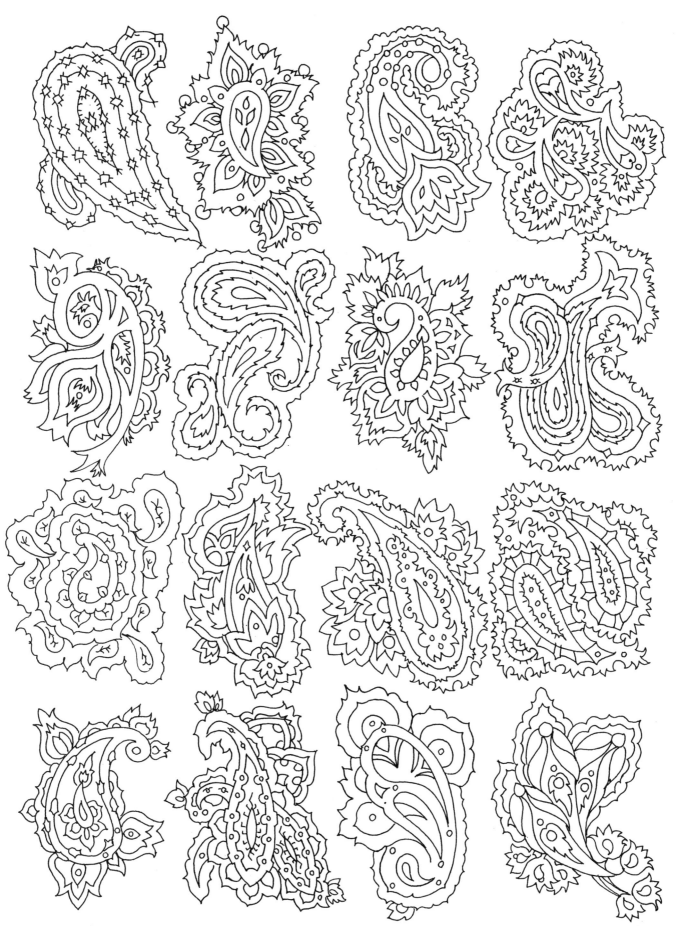

6

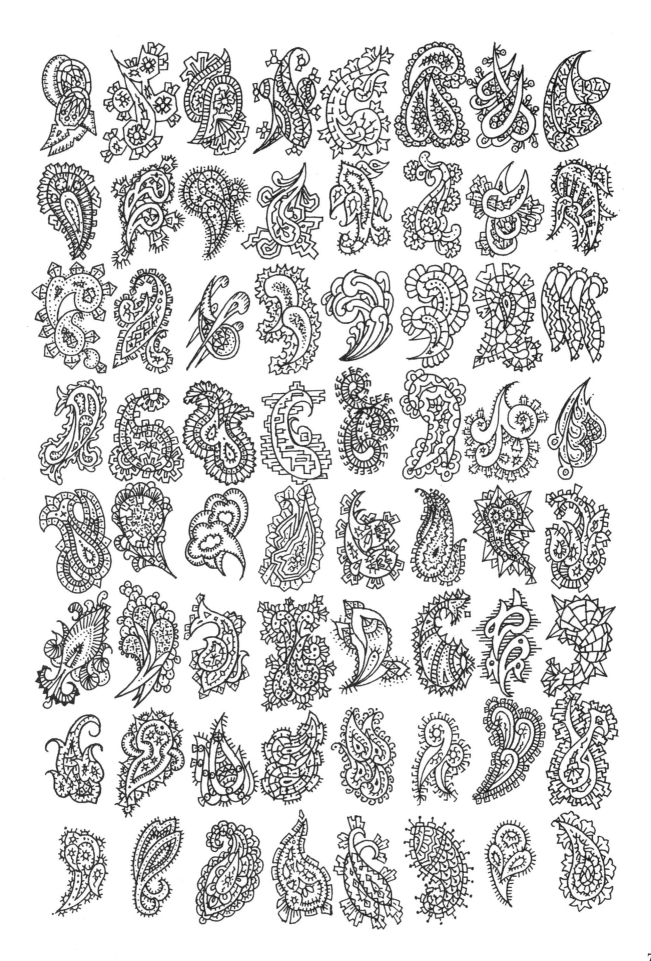

13

14

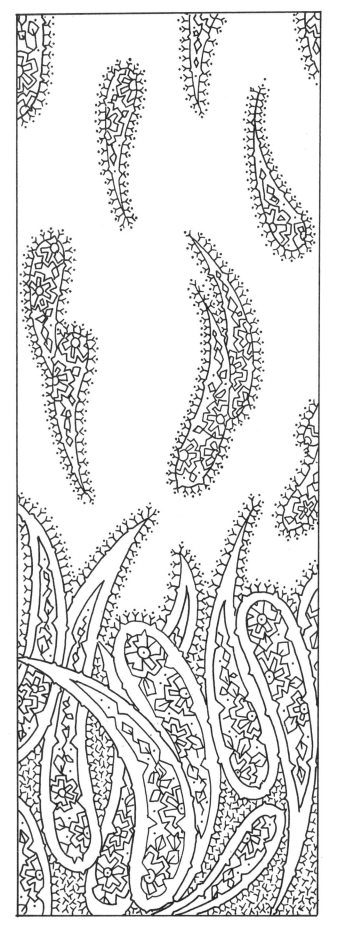

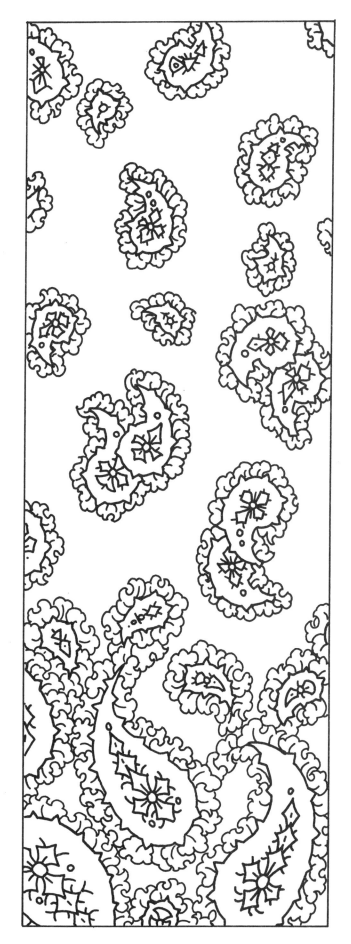

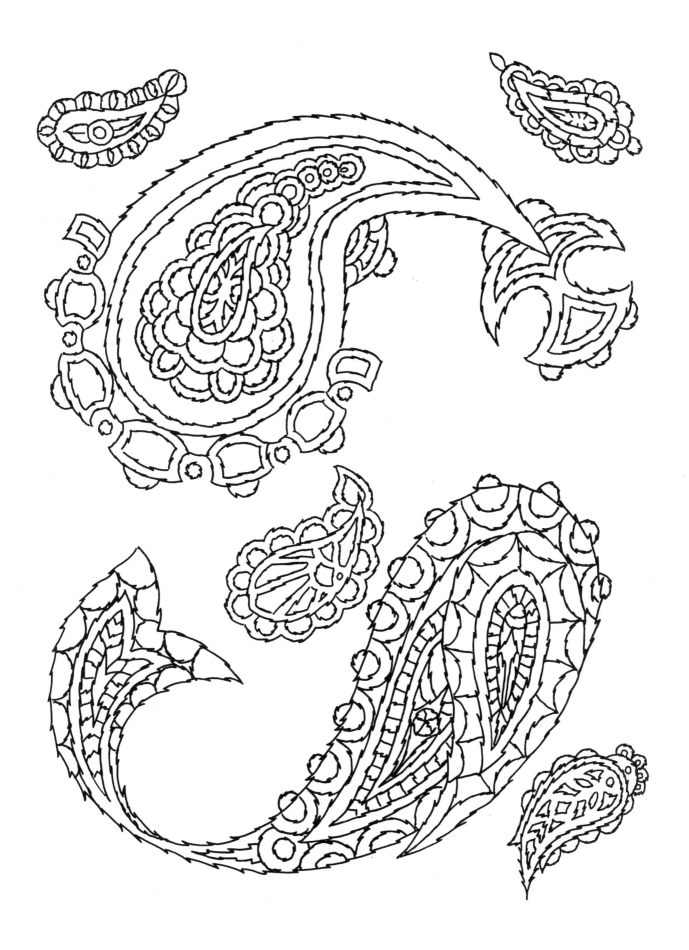

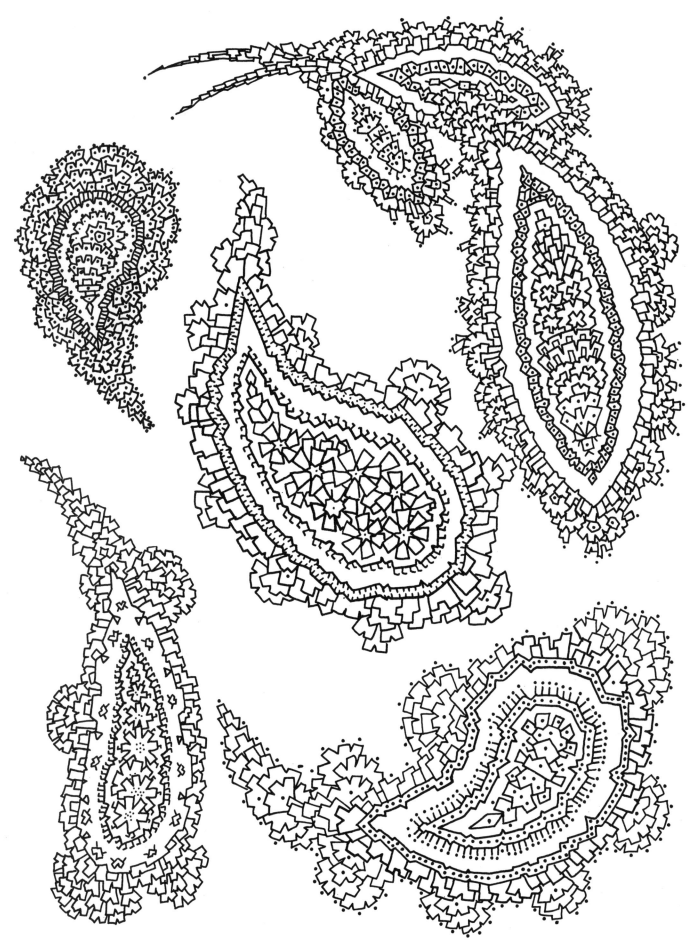

28

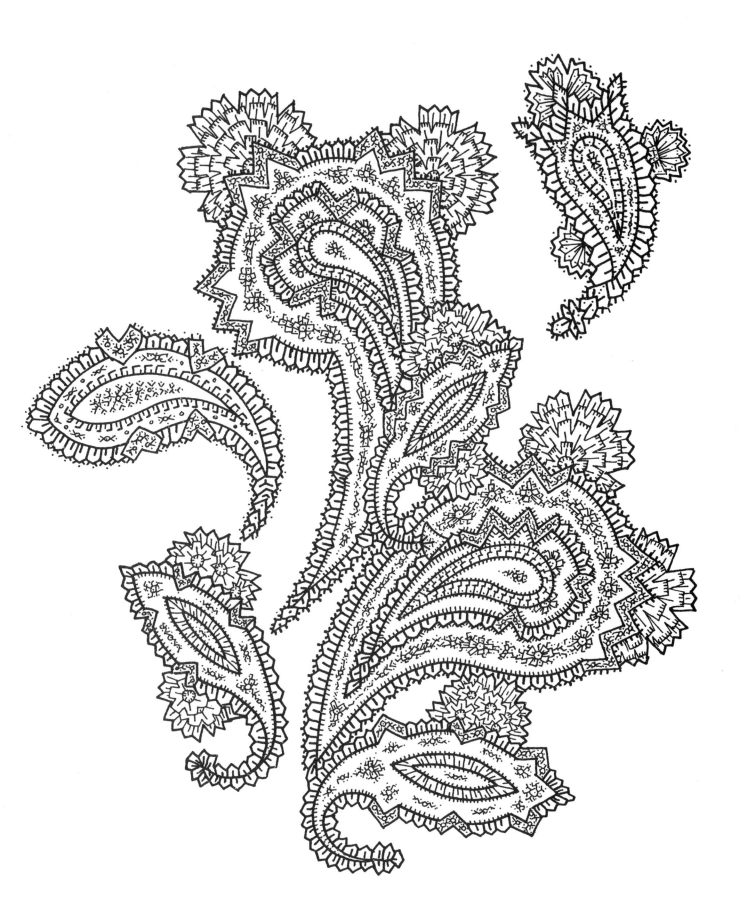

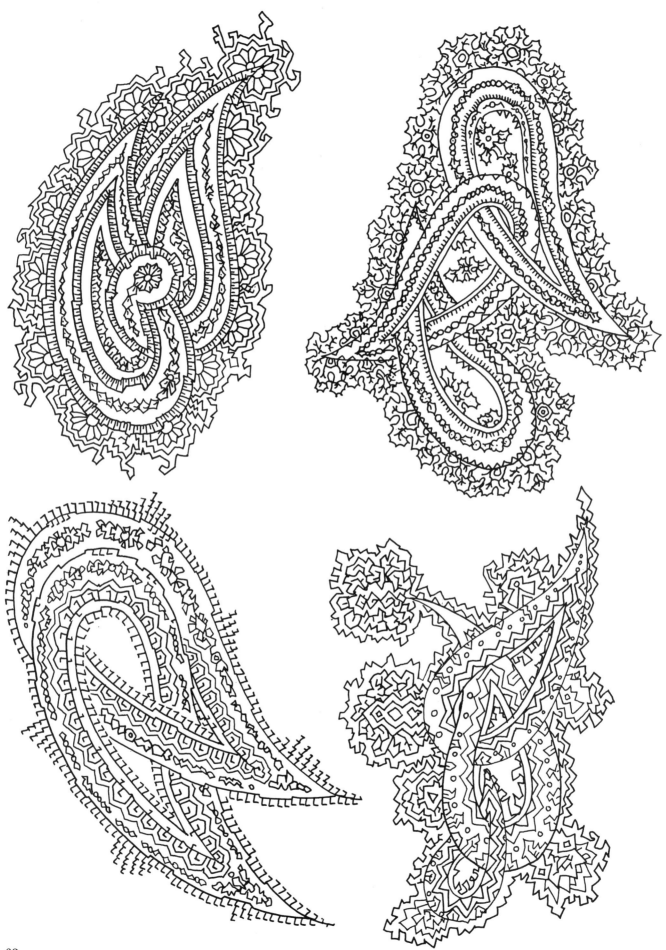

33

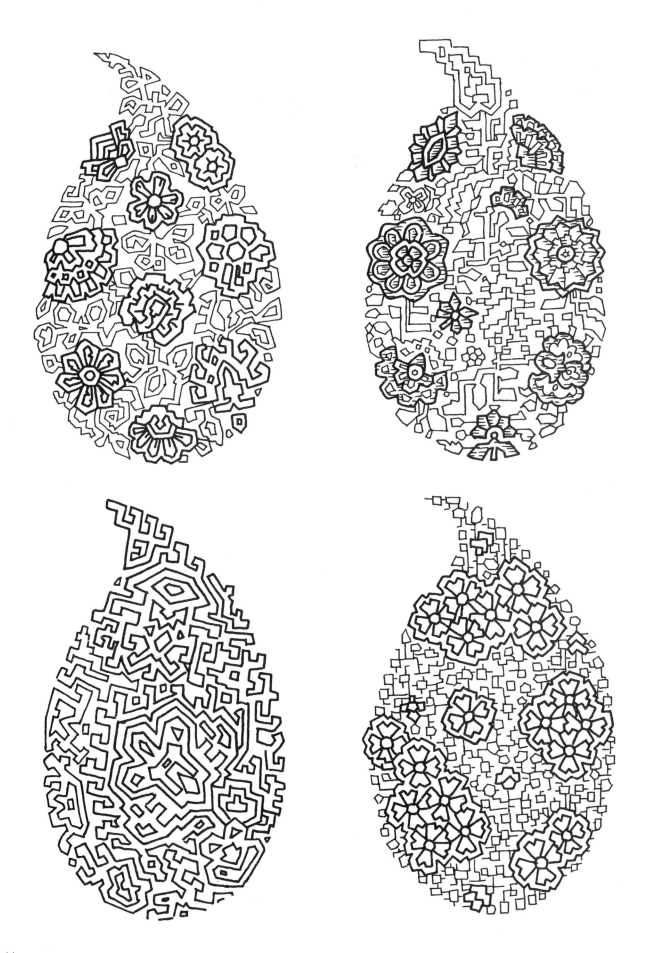

44